ABC'S IN THE LAND OF GLUBBER

RICK POPLINGER

This book is dedicated to my first
grandchild, Aria Raphaela Poplinger

Welcome!

Once upon a time there was a land called Glubber,
And everyone there had a face made of rubber!!

They made all sorts of faces that were funny and merry,
And then they could change them to be ugly and scary!!

But this wasn't the only thing they knew how to do…
These very strange people made some strange noises too!!

They could twist up their rubbery faces till they looked like a dream,
Then all of a sudden, they might let out a big scream!

Then bending their ears and their noses and chins,
While crowing and clucking like old mother hens!!

We never quite knew how they would look every day,
We never quite knew just what they might say!

I shall start a great adventure and you can come too,
To that great land of Glubber, to do the things that they do!!

When they make a strange face, be it oval, square or round,
When they make a strange noise, no matter what that sound,

We will do just like them, oh won't that be great!
It'll be a worthy adventure and I really can't wait:

ANT

Now that we're in Glubber, let's try the first sound.
They want us to talk like that thing on the ground!

But what is that thing, is it not a small ANT??
I don't know how it sounds so I guess I just can't!

But let us just imagine that the ants talk each day,
Use your imagination to tell what they might say!!!

BABOON

Now that was a sound that started us out good,
Now let's do the face that the Glubber said we should.

We will try very hard to make the face that he did,
Even though this is not normally the face of a kid!!

But now that he has shown us, our time will come soon,
To make that strange face that looks like a BABOON!!

COCKLE DOODLE DO

Then we just kept on going, on down the long road,
And then we saw one that was about to explode.

He was pushing and grunting and twisting around,
But even with that effort, he didn't make a sound.

But he kept on trying, even though he turned blue,
Then suddenly it came, it was a COCKLE DOODLE DO!!

DOG

Now this one is hard, but I think we will succeed.
Even though this is a face that we really don't need!

It is a wonderful animal, that we know very well,
He stays at our home. Do you want me to tell??

Well maybe it's a fox, or a horse or a hog...
But maybe you guessed that it's our very own DOG!!

EEEEEEEEEEEEEEEEEEEEEE

EEEEEEEE

Now this one from Glubber was running along.
Screaming out loud something that wasn't a song!

It really did scare me, and he had a strong voice.
Standing close by this one, wasn't really my choice.

It was just one long sound, as high as can be,
He was running and screaming a capital EEEEEE!!!

FAIRY

Hey let's look like that thing, that we see in the sky,
With its buzz and its looks, is it a simple housefly??

But no, this is something else that flies in the air,
It is much better than a fly, I really do swear!

Cause this one is nice and it makes you feel merry,
The face that we'll do next will be the face of that FAIRY!!

GRRRRRRRRRRRRRRR

GRRRRRRR

Now let's do a sound that will wake up the night.
Let us do it so loud, it will cause lots of fright!!

Some animals make this sound, that scares us so much,
Like lions and tigers and animals as such.

The sounds that they make, those animals with fur,
Sound ferocious at night, when you hear a loud GRRRRRR!!

HWAoohhHHHH eeeHHH
Heeee Hawwwwwwwwww

HEE HAW

Well I see that those Glubbers do animal faces,
Like birds in the air and horses in races.

But the noises they make, they're really quite fun,
The growls and the clucks and the others they've done.

Now let us do the sound, of the funniest one we saw,
We'll bray like a donkey with a big loud HEE HAW!!

INSECT

Gosh, what is that sound, buzzing close to my ears?
It sounds much louder, the closer it nears!

It is an INSECT with wings, flying close to my face,
Doing flips in the sky, as it zooms into space!

It can land on a bed or a lamp or a rug,
Let's jump in the air and do the sound of this bug!!!!

JACK – O – LANTERN

Now there is a Glubber who thinks it's Halloween.
He's making a face that looks very mean!

But a Jack-O-Lantern does not have to be bad.
He can have a good face, not one that is sad.

A happy JACK-O-LANTERN, I am sure we can do.
Let's make this good face and let the others scare you!!

KISS

Hey, there are some things that make you feel great!
Together with some actions, that make you can't wait.

There's an action together with this particular sound,
I wish there were more, that we could just pass around.

And I like to get these, from Dad, Mom and Sis,
It's the wonderful sound that comes with a KISS!

LEMON OR LIME

There are several funny faces that make me start giggling,
When you twist up your nose, and start all that wiggling.

When you stand on your head and grab your big lip,
Then twist it around and then down to your hip!

But if you want a sour face, at just any ole time,
Just take a big bite from a LEMON or LIME!

MELODY

You know what we should do, as we continue along?
We should sing to the Glubbers, our very own song!

We can pick one from the songs, that we've all loved so well,
Like "Itsy Bitsy Spider", or the "Farmer in the Dell".

Now let's sing it out so sweet, so that the Glubbers will see,
Just how wonderful it sounds, our favorite MELODY!!

NICE

To sing such a song, for our friends sure is neat,
Friendship is something that you really can't beat!

After all these great songs, and other sounds that we've done,
We should make a nice face, that shows it's been fun.

To double our pleasure, we will make this face twice,
Let's do a wonderful face, that looks very nice!

Oink
Oink
Oink
Oink

OINK

Now I have a riddle, just what makes this call?
It is an animal you know, who's not cute at all.

He wallows in mud, out in the barnyard,
He's really so fat, since he's filled up with lard.

You're right, it's a pig, with curly tail and snout,
He OINKS very loud, when he lets out a shout!!

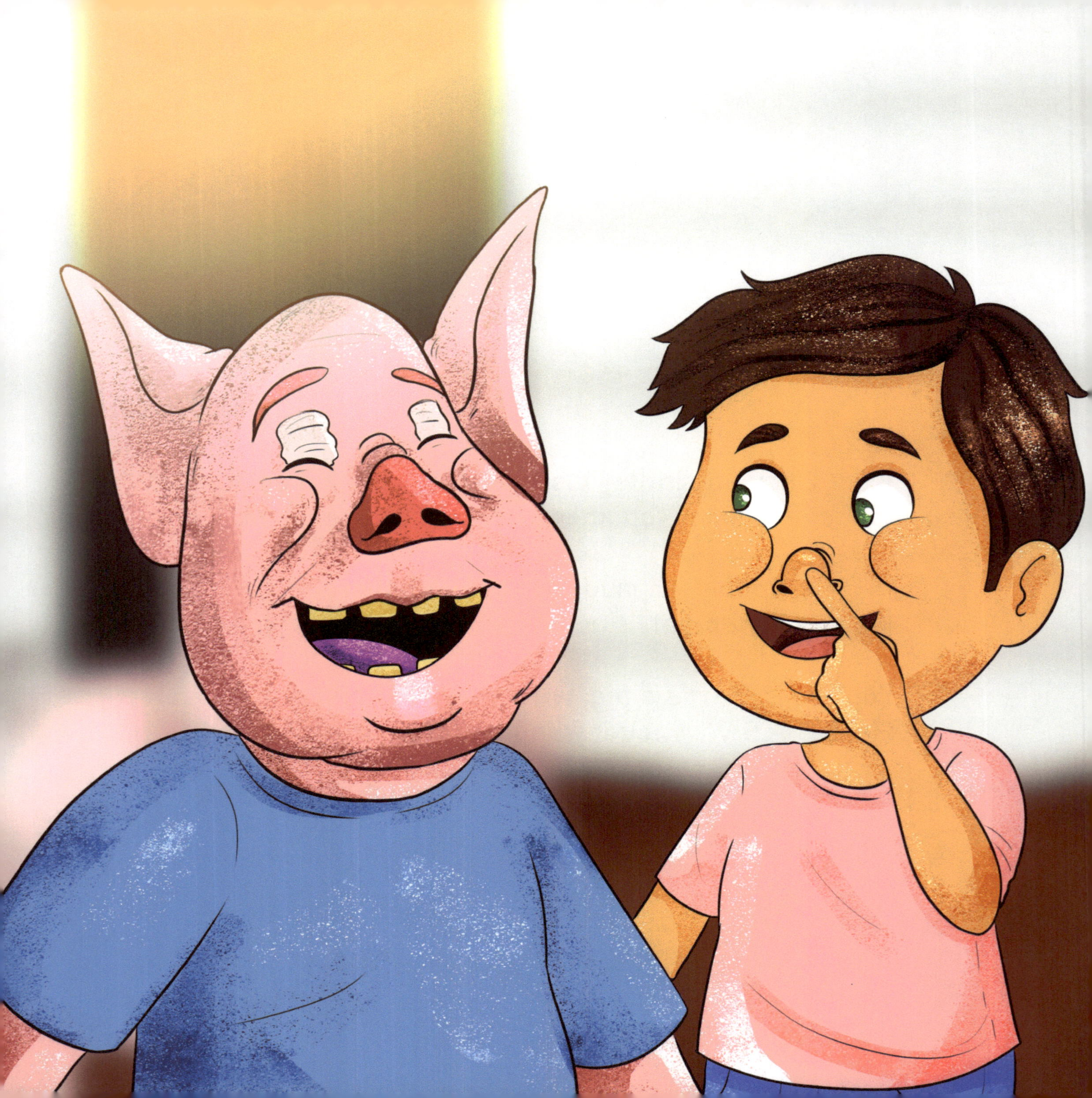

PIG

Along with his oink, let's do his face too,
I'll make his fat snout, now what about you?

To pull up your nose, and puff out your chin,
To look like a hog, in that dirty pigpen.

Should we add some wet mud, since in puddles he digs?
Then we will really look like, those dirty ole PIGS!!

QUACK
Meow!
NEIGHH!

QUACK

With all of these different sounds, we really could confuse,
The animals who wouldn't know whose voice was whose.

Then kitties would whinny, and horses would squeak,
Eagles would meow, and monkeys would speak!

It would be so funny, that we would really jump back,
If the alligators would neigh, and the elephants would
QUACK!!!

RAWRRRRRR!!!!!!

ROAR

That Glubber over there looks like a lion so proud,
And as a big lion he can surely growl loud.

And when I hear him growl, I truly can say,
Let's step to the side and just stay out of his way.

Cause when a lion does talk, it's seldom a bore,
Now let's do it with him, let's let out a big ROAR!!!

SnoreeeeeeeeeeeE

SNORE

Hey, here's a funny sound, my dad often makes,
It rattles the house, like dangerous earthquakes.

It's usually at night, when we're all fast asleep,
When you expect it to be quiet without even a peep.

Then out it comes flying, through dad's bedroom door,
It's his sleepy time melody, that we call a SNORE!!!

TOAD

Making faces is something, we all like to do,
But doing the actions, is quite often fun too!

So the next Glubber we see, we'll act the same way,
Is that all right with you, is it really OK?

Well here comes a Glubber, he's jumping down the road,
Hopping up and down, and making the face of a TOAD!

UGLY

Well now it's our turn, to make a new look,
One that shouldn't ever, be in this good book.

It is one that I must say, that I couldn't take a dare,
To look in a mirror, and not get a big scare!

But I will look anyway, and wonder if it's me...
Can I really make such a face, that is down right UGLY??

VOICE

Do you know what has been great, in this wondrous place?
That everyone loves us, no matter what our face.

And they know we are wonderful, no matter how we sound,
They know that we are great, and guess what we found:

That we love them too, they are the friends of our choice,
So let's yell out our joy, in our loveliest VOICE!

WITCH

After our nice voice, let's try something scary,
To make a strange face, that is ugly and hairy.

But this one is not an animal, as you might have thought,
It rides on a broom, and stirs a big pot.

And while flying on a broom, it rides up in space,
Let's do the next look, like an old WITCH's face!

EXCITED, EXCELLENT, EXTRA!

Boy! Am I eXcited, that we've come all this way,
This is an interesting place, and I'd sure like to stay!

But before we have to go, I would really like to say,
That you are eXcellent kids, just about every ole day.

So hurrah for this adventure, and if we may,
Let's finish up this time, with an eXtra loud yay!!

YIPPEEE I O KAYAY!!!!!

YiPPEE I O KAYAY

We have been having fun, it has really been a ball,
But the day will end soon, and night time will fall.

But with these great memories, we'll come back some time,
It has been nice doing these things, and doing it in rhyme.

So for one of our last sounds, that we will do today,
Let's pucker up those lips, and let out a YIPPEEE I O KAYAY!!!!

ziiiiiiiiipp

ZIPPER

Well that was really great, making those sounds and those faces,
And we met some nice people, and went to nice places.

But it's time to return, so let's go back to the start,
And we will choose one last sound, as a nice way to part.

Let's sound like a ZIPPER, as we finish to roam,
Let's ZIP on back, cause there's no place like home!

GOODBYE

EPILOGUE

Now that we're back, wasn't that quite neat,
To twist up our faces, our bodies and feet!

To be like those Glubbers, in all their delight,
It surely was strange, we were such a strange sight!

And the sounds they were great, a marvel we were,
If I could go there again, I'd go back for sure.

But I would like to tell you something, that you ought to know,
If I could actually twist my face, like this and like so,

I would push it and turn it ... until it would do,
And I am sure at that time, I'd look just like you!

Because you are so wonderful, this had to be said,
So remember that in your dreams, when you're safe in your bed.

THE END

ABOUT THE AUTHOR

Rick Poplinger is a retired water treatment specialist living in Houston, Texas. He is an avid skydiver with over 3500 jumps and several world records. He is a world traveler having been to over 40 countries. He has copyrights on piano compositions as well. This is Rick's second published children's book.